A PICTORIAL GUIDE TO CHEQUE COLLECTING

by
DAVID SHAW

Published by Cheques Unlimited (Regd.)
47 Elm Grove,
NAIRN
Scotland
IV12 4SL

ISBN 0 9510412 0 7

Printed by John G Eccles Printers Ltd, Inverness

CONTENTS

INTRODUCTION

Cheque collecting represents one of the few remaining hobbies where material has not been specifically 'manufactured' to meet known demand. For that very reason it is surprising that so little has been written on the subject until quite recently and even now there are perhaps only a few hundred followers in the whole of Great Britain. It does, however, mean that we have a marvellous opportunity to 'get in on the ground floor' and absorb something of this part of business life which has been around for at least three hundred years.

The humble cheque can form the basis of collections for all manner of enthusiast from those who thrive on its historical angle to the autograph hunter for whom the Victorian cheque can now be seen as an un-tapped source of supply. Similarly cheques of all ages provide another vehicle for the vast army of revenue stamp devotees, not forgetting anyone whose eye may simply be caught by a fine piece of early engraving. Today's opportunities may not be around for very much longer so may I offer this book to those who may wish to take up the challenge for whatever motive.

This volume should be looked on as a companion to my 'COLLECTOR'S GUIDE TO BRITISH CHEQUES' and is aimed, purely and simply, at newcomers to the hobby who may be less inclined, at the outset at least, to seek much in the way of historical detail. The main purpose is therefore merely to give some idea of the already wide range of material which has come on to the market within the last few years. The selection of items which follows represents a small part of my own reference collection built up over a decade and, whilst no attempt could be made at pricing individually, some guidelines are given on page 81.

ACKNOWLEDGEMENTS

Many people have been most helpful in providing me with their advice and thoughts over a lengthy period of time. Personal thanks can be taken to all but I must give special mention to fellow Dealers, Colin Narbeth, Mike Veissid and Trevor Jones, all of whom have given me information as to Collectors' requirements. Discussion is a very valuable tool to an author and I also thank Collectors John Purser, Alistair Gibb and Alan Airey for their kind comments and assistance since this project was first considered.

DAVID SHAW

Fig. 1.   Agra Bank Limited, Nicholas Lane, Lombard Street, London, 1878. *Liquidation 1900.*

Fig. 2.   Jonathan Backhouse & Company, Bankers, Darlington, 1849. *Incorporated as part of Barclay & Company in 1896.*

Fig. 3. Bacon, Cobbold, Tollemache & Co., Ipswich, 1899. *The year they were absorbed by Bacon, Cobbold & Co.*

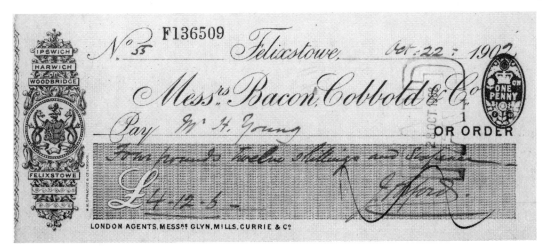

Fig. 4. Bacon, Cobbold & Co., Felixstowe, 1902. *Short-lived title which became part of Capital & Counties Bank network in 1905.*

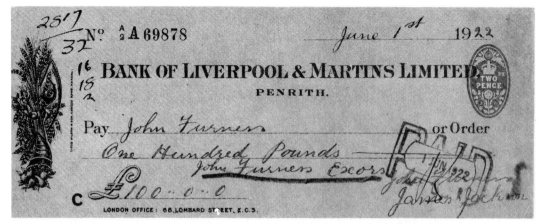

Fig. 5.   Bank of Liverpool & Martins Ltd., Penrith, 1922. *Title shortened to Martins Bank Ltd. in 1928.*

Fig. 6.   The Bank of Mona, Peel, 1877. *A Branch of the ill-fated City of Glasgow Bank opened in the Isle of Man.*

Fig. 7. Bank of Westmorland, Kendal, 1884. *Absorbed by the London & Midland Bank in 1893.*

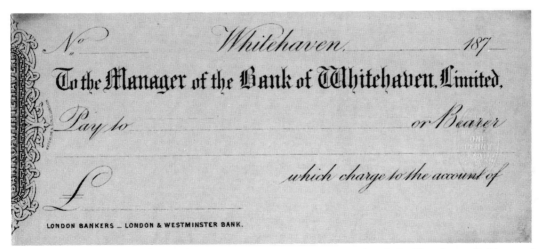

Fig. 8. Bank of Whitehaven Ltd., Whitehaven, 1872. *Amalgamated with the Manchester & Liverpool District Banking Co. in 1916.*

Fig. 9. Barclay, Bevan, Tritton & Co., 54 Lombard Street, London, 1863. *One of several early partnerships for this Bank.*

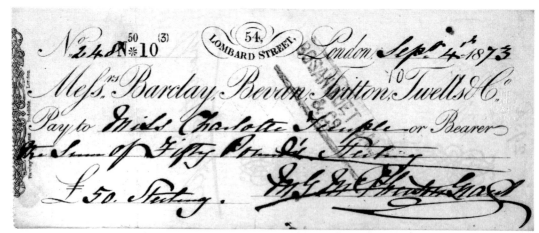

Fig. 10. The above title was changed to Barclay, Bevan, Tritton, Twells & Co., from 1865-1880. *This example dates from 1873.*

Fig. 11.   Eastbourne Bankers, Molineux, Whitfield & Co. *Mentioned on an outstanding pictorial Barclay & Co. item from 1905.*

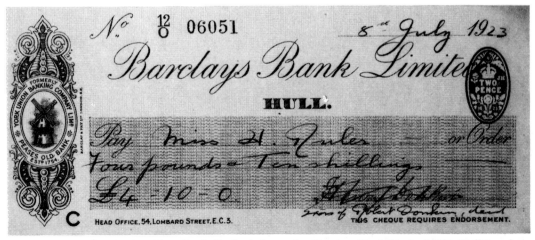

Fig. 12.   By 1917 the title of Barclay & Co. had changed to Barclays Bank Limited. *This Hull item from 1923 re-calls its origins.*

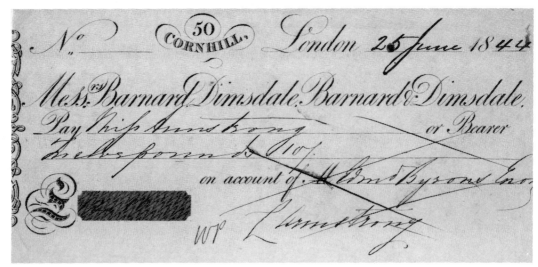

Fig. 13. Barnard, Dimsdale, Barnard & Dimsdale, 50 Cornhill, 1844.

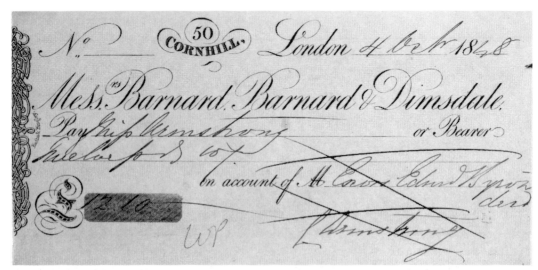

Fig. 14. Similar item from 4 years later in which the title has been reduced to Barnard, Barnard & Dimsdale.

Fig. 15. 62 Lombard Street produced many variations of title for this Lloyds related Bank. 1837, Barnett, Hoare, Hoare & Bradshaw.

Fig. 16. Barnetts, Hoares, Hanburys & Lloyd, 1868. *Became part of Lloyds, Barnetts & Bosanquets Bank in 1884.*

Fig. 17. Yeovil Bankers Edmund Batten & John Batten 1833. *Absorbed by Stuckey's Banking Co. in 1849.*

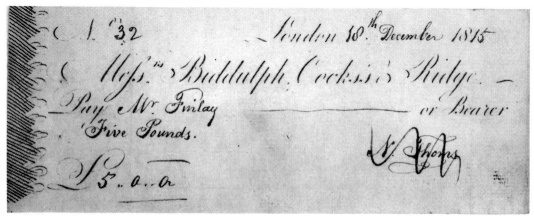

Fig. 18. Biddulph, Cocks's & Ridge, London, 1815. *One of many partnerships for this Bank which eventually passes to Barclays.*

Fig. 19. Boldero, Carter, Barnston & Snaith, London, 1768. *Stopped payment in 1829 when they were known as Sikes, Snaith & Snaith.*

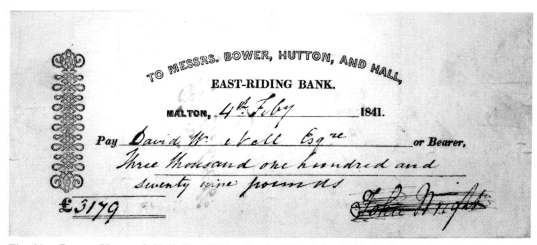

Fig. 20. Bower, Hutton & Hall, East Riding Bank, 1841. *Joined with Beckett & Co. of Leeds in 1875.*

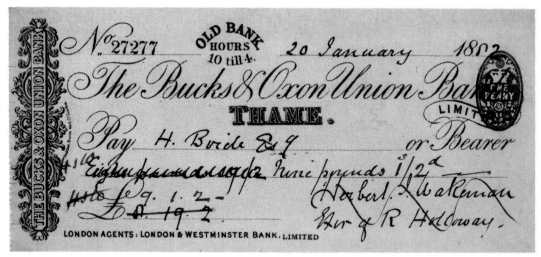

Fig. 21. The Bucks & Oxon Union Bank Limited, Thame, 1882. *Another addition for Lloyds, two years later in 1902.*

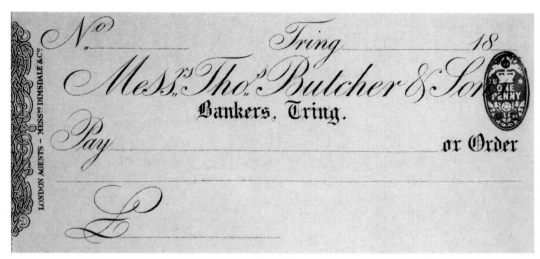

Fig. 22. Thos Butcher & Sons, Tring, 1889. *Amalgamated with Prescott, Dimsdale, Cave, Tugwell & Co. in 1900.*

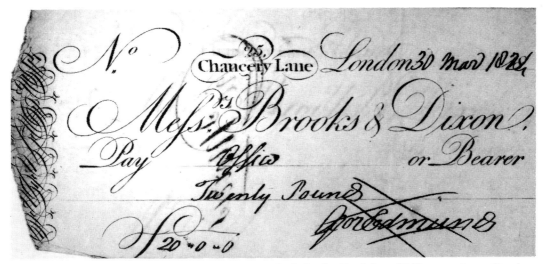

Fig. 23.   Brooks & Dixon. *One of several changes of title for this Bank from 25 Chancery Lane, London, 1824.*

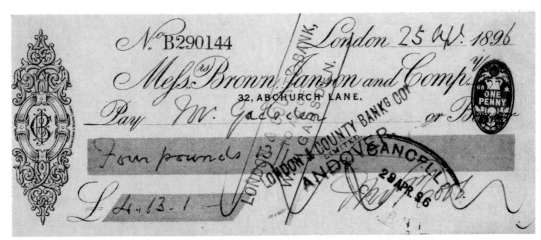

Fig. 24.   Brown, Janson & Compy, 32 Abchurch Lane, London, 1896. *Part of Lloyds Bank network from 1900.*

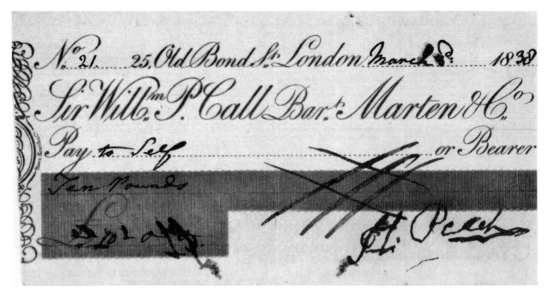

Fig. 25. Sir Willm P Call Bart. Marten & Co., 25 Old Bond Street, London, 1838. *Passes to Herries, Farquhar & Co. in 1865.*

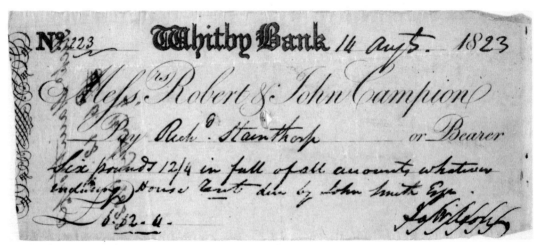

Fig. 26. Robert & John Campion, Whitby Bank, 1823. *Failed in 1841.*

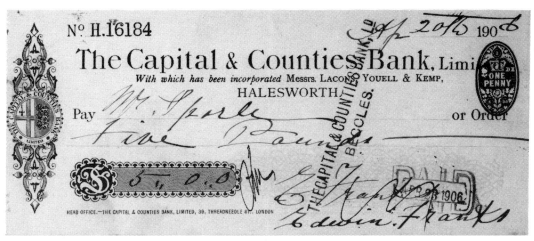

Fig. 27. The Capital & Counties Bank Limited, Halesworth, 1906. *This one includes reference to former Bankers, Lacons, Youell & Kemp.*

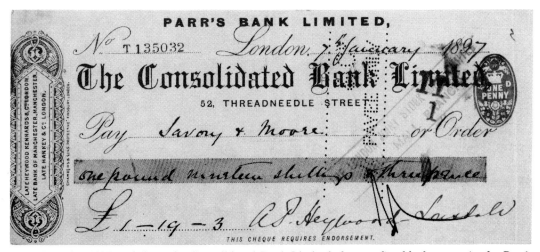

Fig. 28. *This 1897 item from the* Consolidated Bank Limited *shows a fine black over-print for* Parr's Bank.

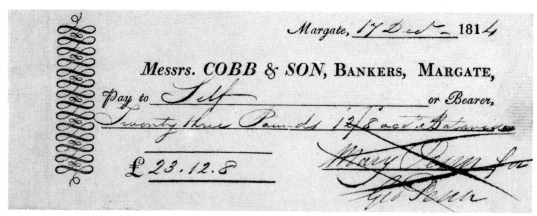

Fig. 29. Cobb & Son, Bankers of Margate. *This example dates from 1814.*

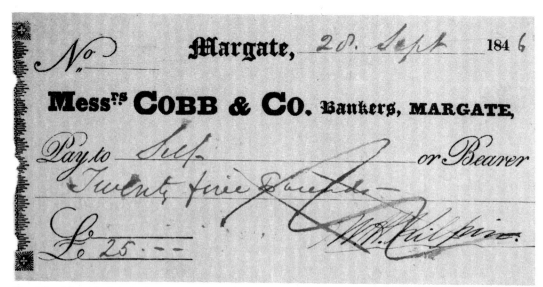

Fig. 30. The title is not often seen as Cobb & Co. as in the above item from 1846. *Taken over by Lloyds Bank in 1891.*

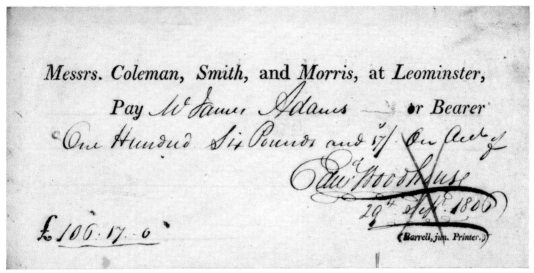

Fig. 31.   Coleman, Smith and Morris, at Leominster, 1806. *Failed 1826.*

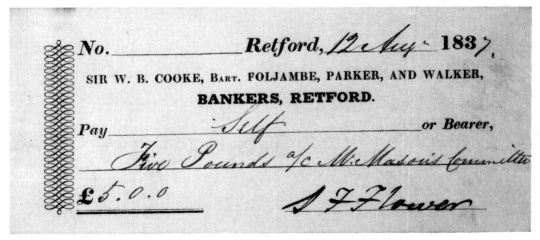

Fig. 32.   Sir W B Cooke, Bart., Foljambe, Parker and Walker, 1837, from Retford. *Scarce Private Bankers.*

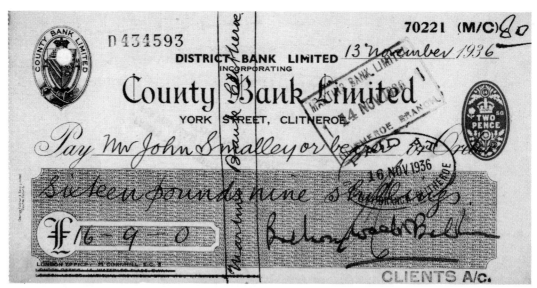

Fig. 33. County Bank Limited, Clitheroe, 1936, showing black over-print for District Bank, following takeover a year earlier.

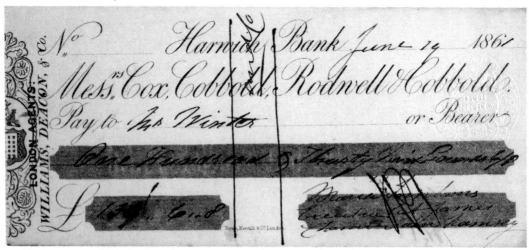

Fig. 34. Cox, Cobbold, Rodwell & Cobbold, Harwich, 1861. *Related to Fig. 3, following takeover in 1893.*

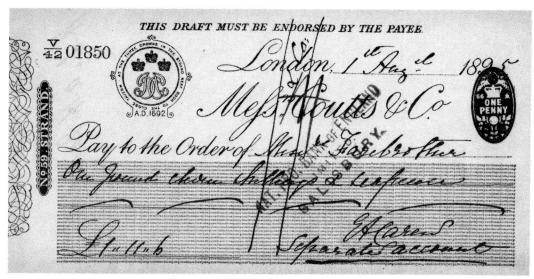

Fig. 35. Coutts & Co., 59 Strand, London, 1895. *Famous Private Bankers found as far back as Thomas Coutts, London Goldsmith.*

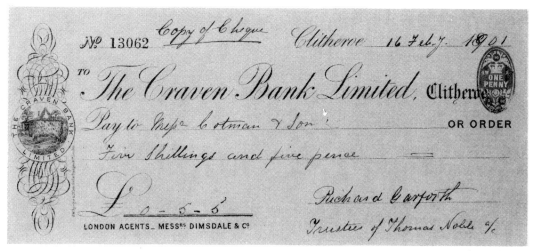

Fig. 36. The Craven Bank Limited, Clitheroe, 1901. *Amalgamated with the Bank of Liverpool in 1906.*

Fig. 37. The Cripplegate Bank, Limited, 31 Whitecross Street, London, 1891.

Fig. 38. Crompton & Evans Union Bank Limited, Bakewell, 1904. *Known as Scarsdale & High Peak Bank, based around Derby.*

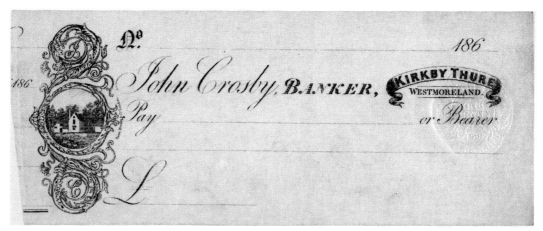

Fig. 39. This 1860 cheque shows a title of John Crosby, Banker, Kirkby Thure.

Fig. 40. The Cumberland Union Banking Co. Limited, Whitehaven 1869. *This one makes reference to recent absorption of Joseph Monkhouse Head & Co., Private Bankers in Carlisle.*

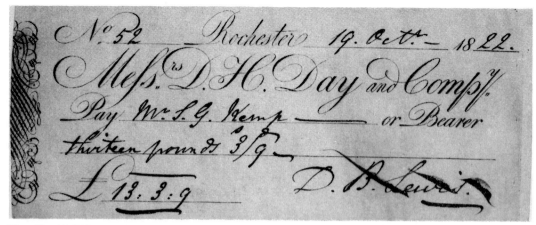

Fig. 41. D H Day and Compy, 1822. *Private Bankers of Rochester and Chatham in Kent.*

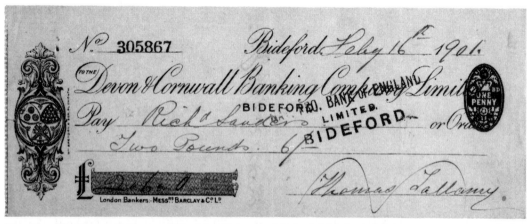

Fig. 42. The Devon & Cornwall Banking Company Limited, Bideford, 1906. *A very popular collecting area this!*

Fig. 43. Dimsdale, Drewett, Fowlers & Barnard, 50 Cornhill, 1860. *Related by amalgamation to Figs. 13 & 14.*

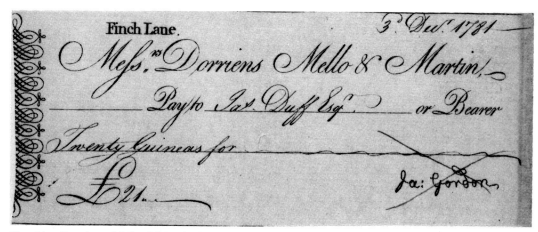

Fig. 44. Dorriens, Mello & Martin, Finch Lane, London, 1781. *Several title changes for this Bank before absorption by Curries & Co. in 1842.*

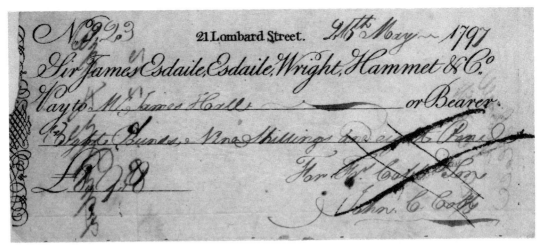

Fig. 45. Sir James, Esdaile, Esdaile, Wright, Hammet & Co., 21 Lombard Street, London, 1797.

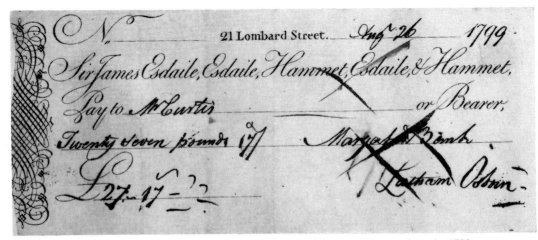

Fig. 46. Sir James Esdaile, Esdaile, Hammet, Esdaile, & Hammet, 2 years later in 1799.

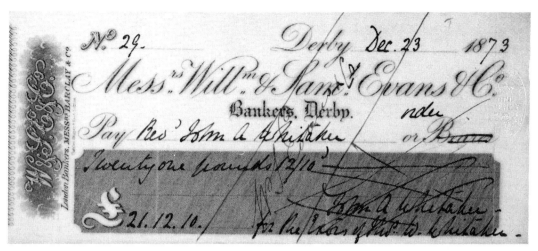

Fig. 47. Willm. & Saml. Evans & Co., Derby, 1873. *Amalgamated with Crompton, Newton & Co. in 1877. See Fig. 38.*

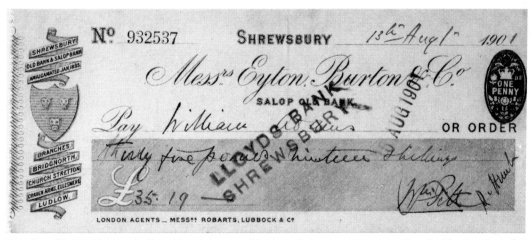

Fig. 48. Eyton, Burton & Co., Shrewsbury, 1901. *One of the numerous units absorbed by the Capital & Counties Bank.*

Fig. 49. Messrs. I G Fordham & Sons, Royston, 1843.

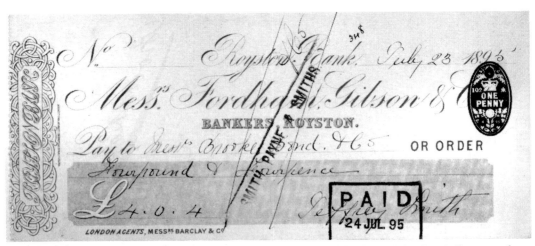

Fig. 50. Title changes from last to Fordham, Gibson & Co. in 1883. *Part of Barclay & Company from 1896.*

Fig. 51. Fox Brothers, Fowler & Co., private Bankers, Barnstaple, 1888.

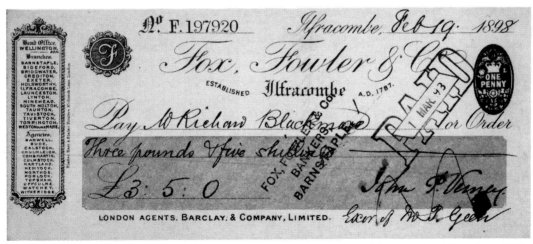

Fig. 52. The above title more well known as Fox, Fowler & Co., this example dating from 1898. *Absorbed by Lloyds Bank in 1921.*

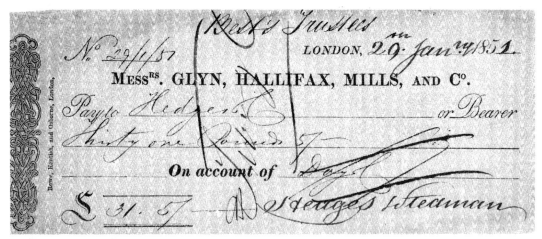

Fig. 53. Glyn, Hallifax, Mills and Co., London, 1854.

Fig. 54. Title changed to Glyn, Mills, Currie & Co., from 1864. *The above example dates from 1890.*

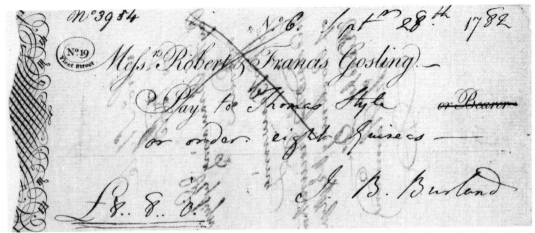

Fig. 55. Robert & Francis Gosling, 1782. *Famous Private Bankers from 19 Fleet Street, London. Many partnerships exist.*

Fig. 56. The name of Goslings & Sharpe lasted from 1794-1896 when it became part of Barclay & Company.

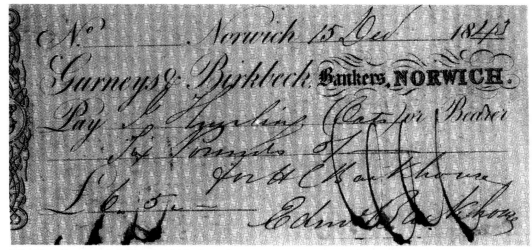

Fig. 57. Gurneys & Birbeck, 1843. *One of numerous partnership changes for this Norwich based Bank.*

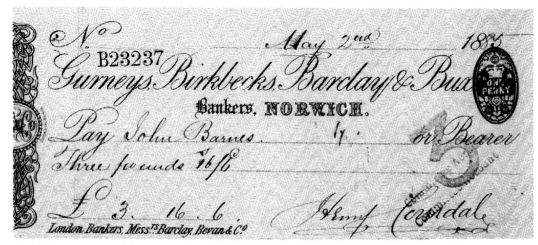

Fig. 58. Gurneys, Birbecks, Barclay & Buxton, 1885. *Another change of title!*

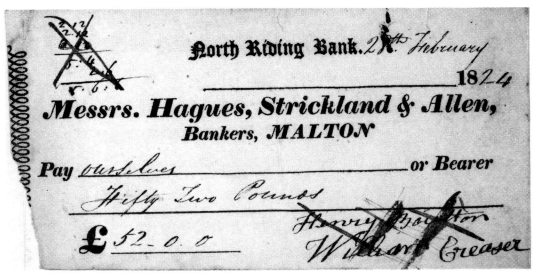

Fig. 59. Hagues, Strickland & Allen, Malton, 1824. *A rare title which went bust in 1826.*

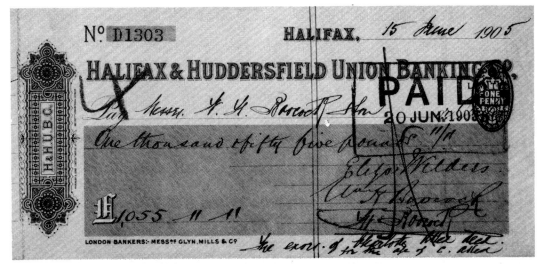

Fig. 60. Halifax & Huddersfield Union Banking Co. Limited, 1905.

Fig. 61. The Brighton Union Bank underwent many title changes — Hall, Lloyd & Bevan, 1861.

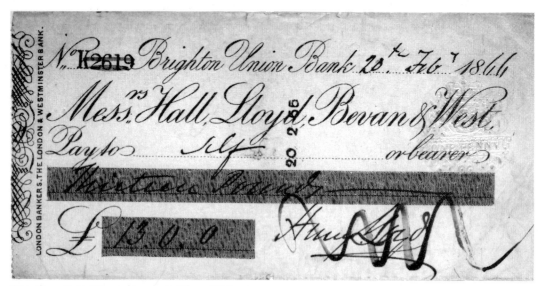

Fig. 62. Hall, Lloyd, Bevan & West, 1866.

Fig. 63. Hammersleys & Co., 69 Pall Mall, London, 1831. *Another of the many Banks which failed, this one finished in 1840.*

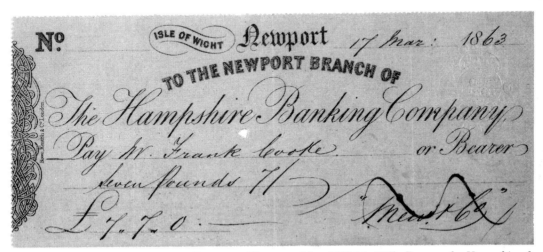

Fig. 64. The Hampshire Banking Company, Newport, Isle of Wight, 1863. *Became the Hampshire & North Wilts Banking Co. in 1877.*

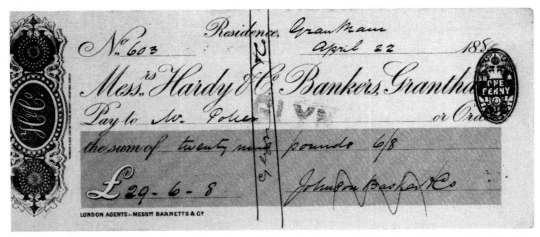

Fig. 65. Hardy & Co., Bankers, Grantham, 1884. *Amalgamated with the Leicester-shire Banking Company in 1895.*

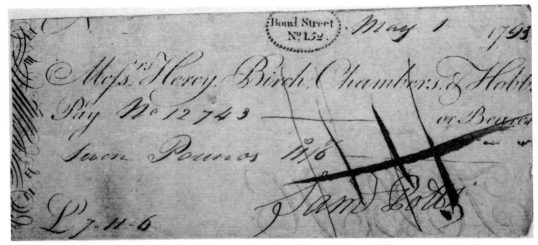

Fig. 66. Hercy, Birch, Chambers & Hobbs, No. 152 Bond Street, London, 1793. *Established 1769, stopped payment in 1824.*

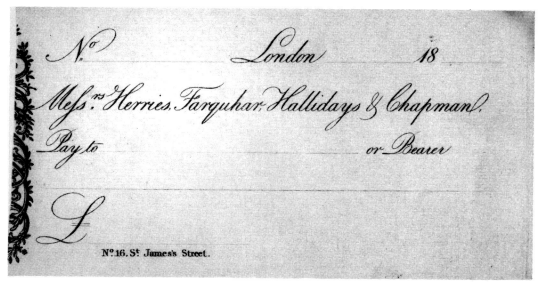

Fig. 67. Herries, Farquhar, Hallidays & Chapman, 16 St. James's Street, London, c.1830.

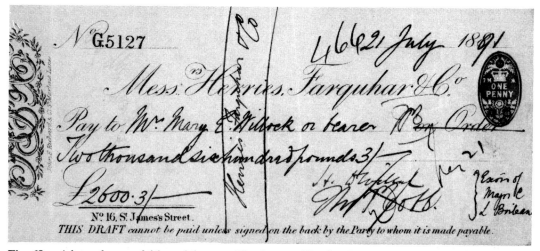

Fig. 68. A later change of title and the same Firm became Herries, Farquhar & Co. *Lloyds Bank related.*

Nº _____   *Liverpool,* _____ 185

Messrs. ARTHUR HEYWOOD, SONS & CO.

On demand pay _____ *or Bearer,*

_____

_____

£ _____

Fig. 69. Arthur Heywood, Sons & Co., Liverpool, c. 1850's. *Amalgamated with the Bank of Liverpool in 1883.*

Fig. 70. Heywood, Kennards & Co., No. 4 Lombard Street, London, 1858. *Amalgamated with Bank of Manchester in 1863 to form the Consolidated Bank.*

Fig. 71. Hilton, Rigden & Rigden, Bankers, Faversham, 1897. *One of the few Kent Banks to have come on the market.*

Fig. 72. Private Bankers Messrs. Hoare, 1889. *Can be traced back to 17th C. Goldsmith's days. Note the vignette of 'leather bottle'.*

Fig. 73. Holt & Co., London, 1916, based on former Bankers Woodheads' Branch. *Absorbed by Glyn, Mills, Currie & Co. in 1923.*

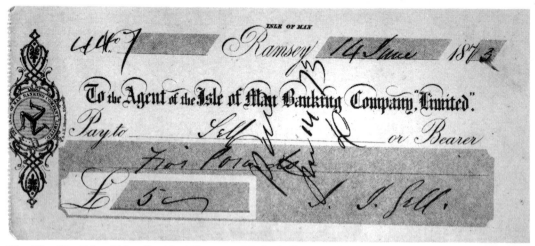

Fig. 74. The Isle of Man Banking Company Limited, Ramsey, 1873.

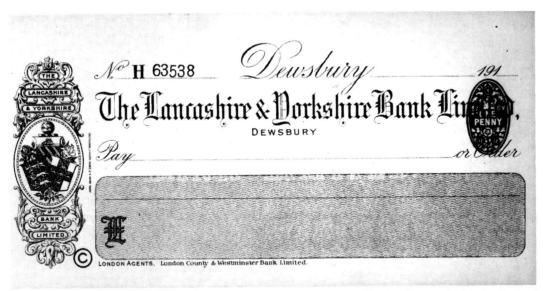

Fig. 75. The Lancashire & Yorkshire Bank Limited, Dewsbury, 1912. *Amalgamated with the Bank of Liverpool & Martins in 1928.*

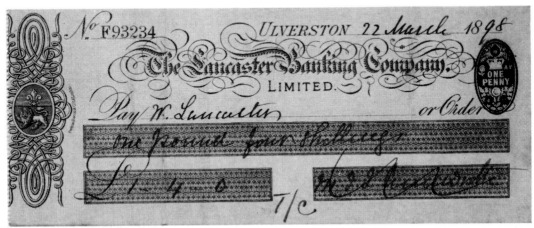

Fig. 76. The Lancaster Banking Company Limited, Ulverston, 1898. *The earliest English Bank to be formed on 'Joint Stock' lines.*

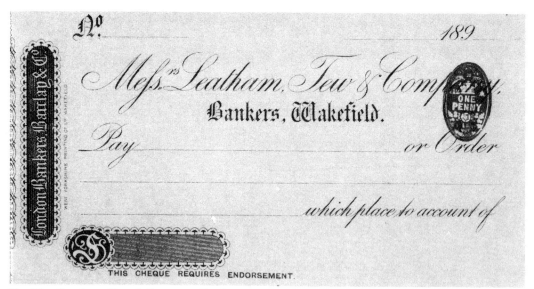

Fig. 77. Leatham, Tew & Company, Bankers, Wakefield, 1897. *Part of the Barclay & Co. network from 1900.*

Fig. 78. The Leeds & County Bank Limited, Wakefield, 1874. *Business taken over by the Birmingham & Midland Bank in 1890.*

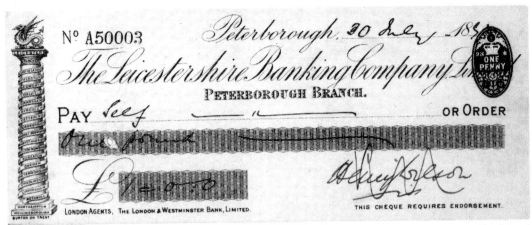

Fig. 79. The Leicestershire Banking Company Limited, Peterborough, 1892. *Part of the Midland Bank network.*

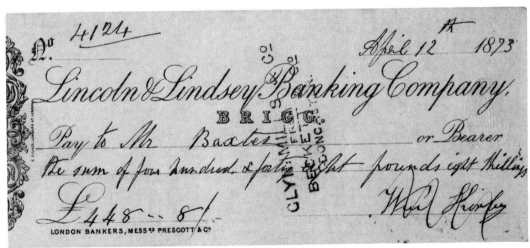

Fig. 80. Lincoln & Lindsey Banking Company, Brigg, 1873. *Amalgamated with the London City & Midland Bank in 1913.*

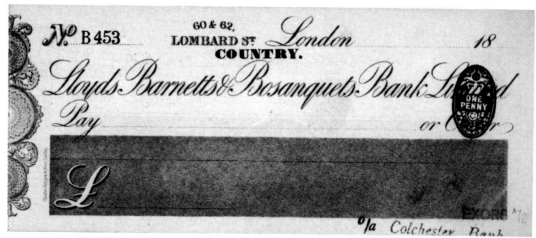

Fig. 81. Lloyds, Barnetts & Bosanquets Bank Limited, 60 & 62 Lombard Street, London, 1886. *See Fig. 16.*

Fig. 82. Sir John William Lubbock, Bart., Forster & Compy., No. 11 Mansion House Place, London, 1849. *Became known as Roberts, Lubbock & Co. from 1860 amalgamation.*

Fig. 83. The London & Midland Bank Limited, Brighton, 1898. *Forerunner of todays Midland Bank.*

Fig. 84. London & County Bank, Chatham, 1867. *One of the main 'arms' of todays National Westminster Bank.*

Fig. 85. Masterman, Peters, Mildred, Masterman & Co., 35 Nicholas Lane, London, 1856. *Suspended payment in 1866 following several changes of title.*

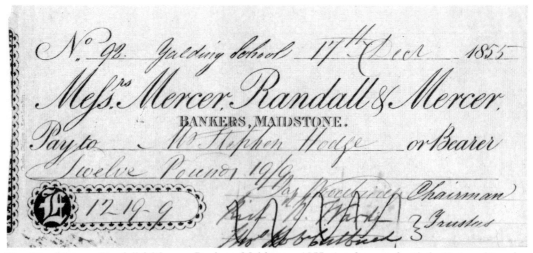

Fig. 86. Mercer, Randall & Mercer, Bankers, Maidstone, 1855. *Amalgamated with the Union of London & Smiths Bank in 1903.*

Fig. 87. The North Eastern Banking Company Limited, Stockton on Tees, 1900. *Eventually passes to the Bank of Liverpool.*

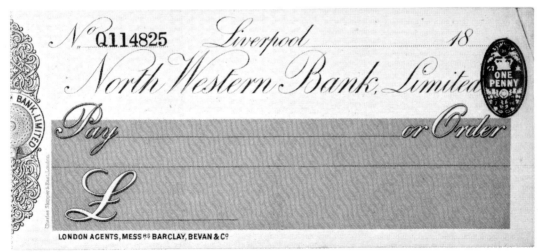

Fig. 88. Its counterpart in name — the North Western Bank Limited, 1894 from Liverpool became Midland Bank related from 1897.

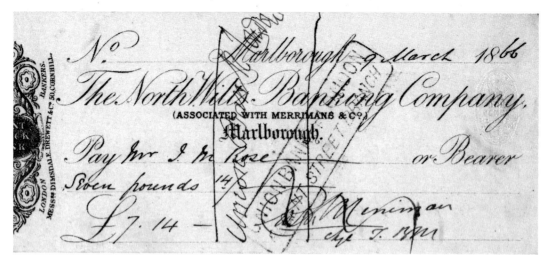

Fig. 89. The North Wilts Banking Company, Marlborough, 1866, including a reference to former Bankers Merriman & Co. *See Fig. 64.*

Fig. 90. The Nottingham Joint Stock Bank Limited, Nottingham, 1889. *Amalgamated with the London City & Midland Bank in 1905.*

Fig. 91. Olding, Sharpe & Co., 29 Clements Lane, London, 1861. *Failed in 1866, after two further changes of title.*

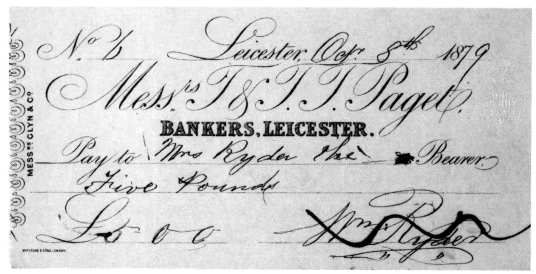

Fig. 92. Messrs. T & T T Paget, Bankers, Leicester, 1879. *Absorbed by Lloyds Bank network in 1895.*

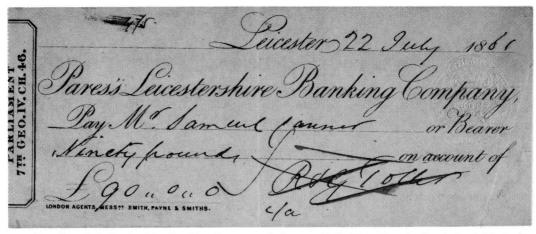

Fig. 93. Pares's Leicestershire Banking Company, Leicester, 1861. *Taken over by Parr's Bank Limited in 1902.*

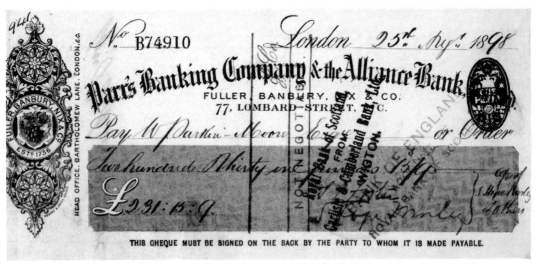

Fig. 94. Parr's Banking Company & The Alliance Bank Limited, 77 Lombard Street, 1898.

Fig. 95. Pedder & Company, Preston Old Bank, c.1850's. *Another failure, this Bank disappearing in 1861.*

Fig. 96. Praed, Fane, Praed & Johnston, 189 Fleet Street, London, 1846. *Absorbed by Lloyds Bank in 1891.*

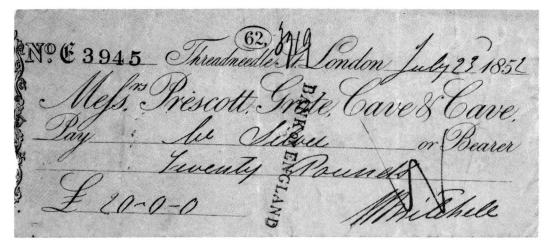

Fig. 97. Prescott, Grote, Cave & Cave, 62 Threadneedle Street, London. *An early partnership, later to become Prescott's Bank Ltd.*

Fig. 98. Almost all cheques for Prescott's Bank Limited, will be found with an over-print for the Union of London & Smith's Bank as the original title only lasted a few months in 1903.

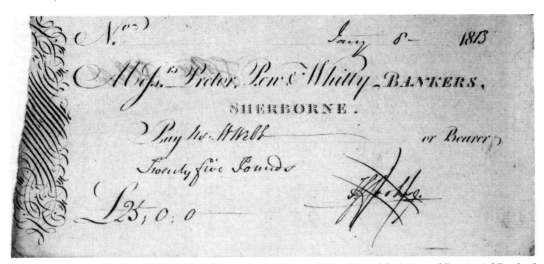

Fig. 99 Messrs, Preter, Pew & Whitty, Bankers, Sherborne, 1813. *Part of the National Provincial Bank of England from 1843.*

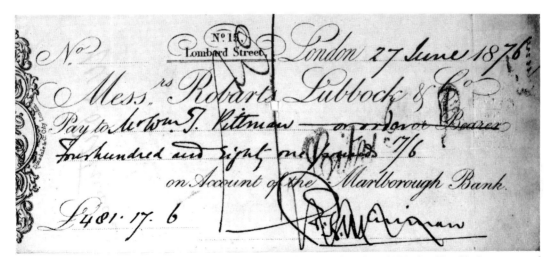

Fig. 100. Robarts, Lubbock & Co., No. 15, Lombard Street, London, 1876. *See Fig. 82. Incorporated with Coutts & Co. in 1914.*

Fig. 101. Seymour, Lamb, Brooks & Hillier, Bankers, Basingstoke, 1850. *Business acquired by the Hampshire Banking Co. in 1864.*

Fig. 102. Sharples, Tuke, Lucas & Lucas, Bankers, Hitchin, 1868.

Fig. 103. Sheffield Banking Company, 1838. *Amalgamated with the National Provincial and Union Bank of England in 1919.*

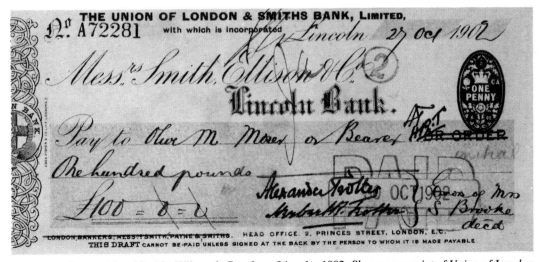

Fig. 104. Scarce title of Smith, Ellison & Co., from Lincoln, 1902. *Shows over-print of Union of London & Smiths Bank at top.*

Fig. 105. Smith, Payne & Smiths, No. 1. Lombard Street, London, 1876.

Fig. 106. Sparrow, Tufnell & Co., Bankers, Chelmsford, 1887. *One of the 20 Banks which formed Barclay & Company in 1896.*

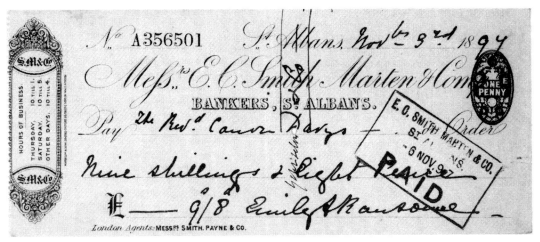

Fig. 107. Messrs. EC Smith, Marten & Compy., Bankers, St. Albans, 1897. *A year later the title became Marten, Part & Co.*

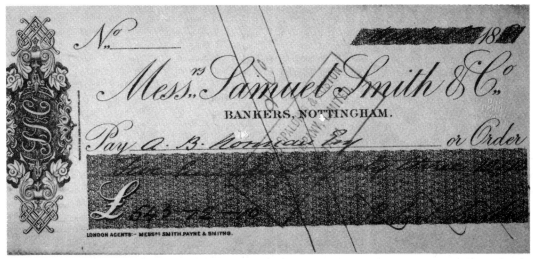

Fig. 108. Samuel Smith & Co., Bankers, Nottingham, 1881. *Merged in the Union of London & Smiths Bank in 1902.*

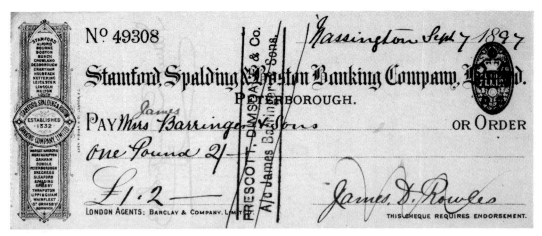

Fig. 109.   Stamford, Spalding & Boston Banking Company Limited, Peterborough, 1897. *Acquired by Barclay & Co. in 1911.*

Fig. 110.   Stephens, Blandy & Co., Reading, 1883. *Taken over by Lloyds Bank in 1899.*

Fig. 111. To Stuckey's Banking Compy., Bath, 1883. *Important west country network, part of the National Westminster Bank group.*

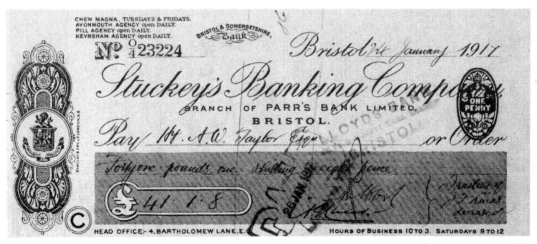

Fig. 112. Such was the importance of Stuckey's Banking Company its title takes first place in this 1917 cheque of Parr's Bank!.

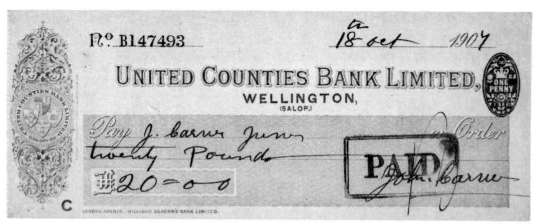

Fig. 113. United Counties Bank Limited, Wellington, 1907. *Amalgamated with Barclay & Company in 1916.*

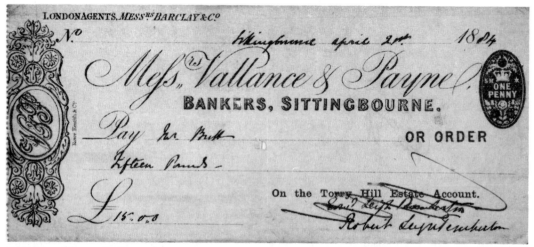

Fig. 114. Messrs, Vallance & Payne, Bankers, Sittingbourne, 1884. *Became part of Martin & Co. 4 years later.*

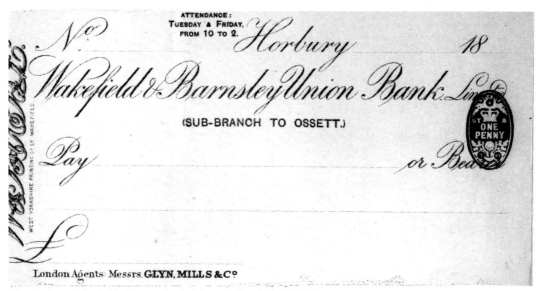

Fig. 115. Wakefield & Barnsley Union Bank Limited, Horbury, 1889. *Taken over by the Birmingham District & Counties Banking Co. in 1906.*

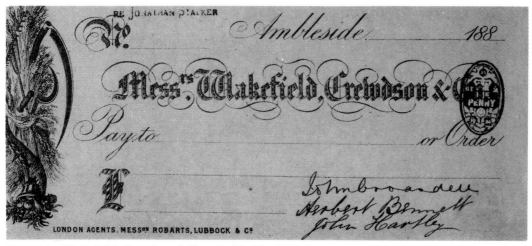

Fig. 116. Wakefield, Crewdson & Co., Ambleside, 1886. *Became part of the Bank of Liverpool in 1893.*

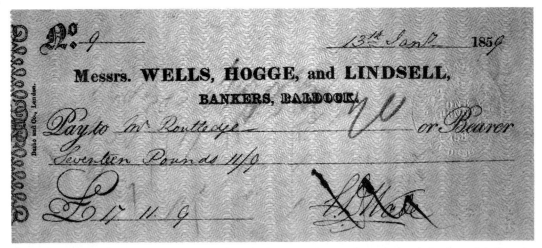

Fig. 117. Wells, Hogge and Lindsell, Bankers, Baldock, 1859. *Amalgamated with the Capital & Counties Bank in 1893.*

Fig. 118. The West of England & South Wales District Bank, Bideford, 1875. *Failed in 1878.*

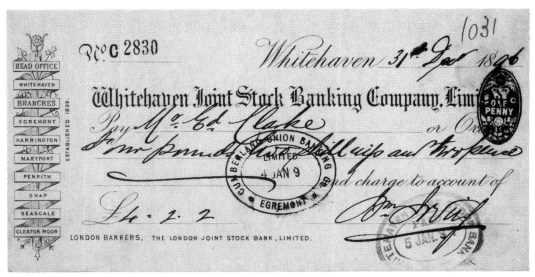

Fig. 119. Whitehaven Joint Stock Banking Company Limited, Whitehaven, 1896. *Amalgamated with Parr's Bank in 1908.*

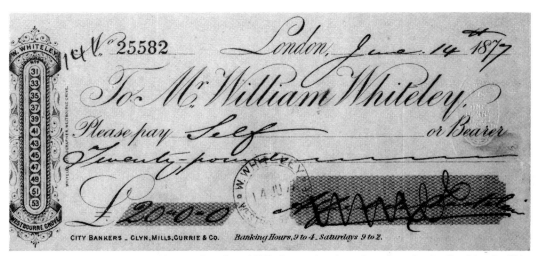

Fig. 120. To Mr William Whiteley, London, 1877. *Interesting item thought to be for Banking facilities within Whiteley's Stores.*

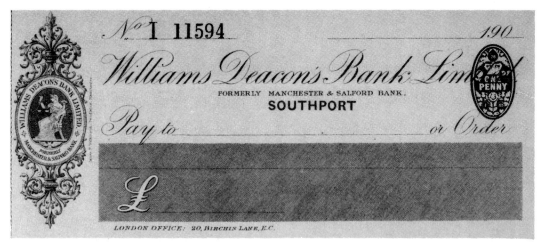

Fig. 121. Williams Deacons Bank Limited, Southport, 1905, showing a recently taken over unit, the Manchester & Salford Bank.

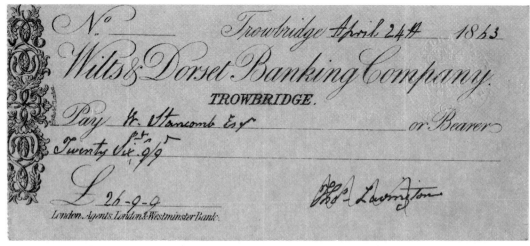

Fig. 122. Wilts & Dorset Banking Company, Trowbridge, 1863. *Amalgamated with Lloyds Bank in 1914.*

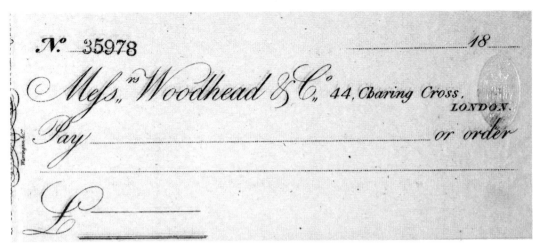

Fig. 123. Messrs. Woodhead & Co., 44 Charing Cross, London. *Taken over by Holt & Co. in 1915. See Fig. 73.*

Fig. 124. Messrs. Woods & Compy., Newcastle on Tyne, 1896. *Amalgamated with Barclay & Company a year later.*

Fig. 125.   Messrs. J & J C Wright, Nottingham, 1865. *Amalgamated with the Capital & Counties Bank in 1898.*

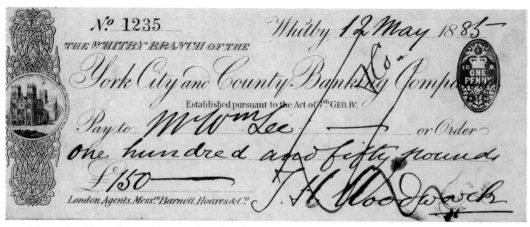

Fig. 126.   The York City and County Banking Company, Whitby, 1885. *Fine example from a series which includes some spectacular pictorial vignettes of Cathedrals and Abbeys.*

Fig. 127. Yorkshire Banking Compy, Pontefract, 1859. *Amalgamated with the London City & Midland Bank in 1901.*

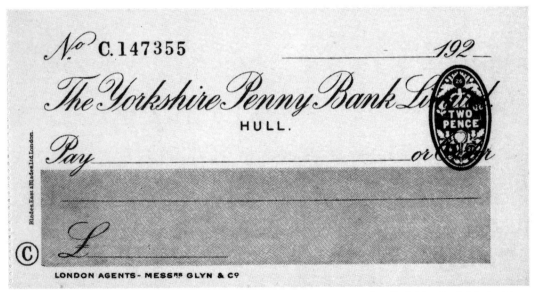

Fig. 128. The Yorkshire Penny Bank Limited, Hull, 1928. *Title changed to Yorkshire Bank Limited from 1959.*

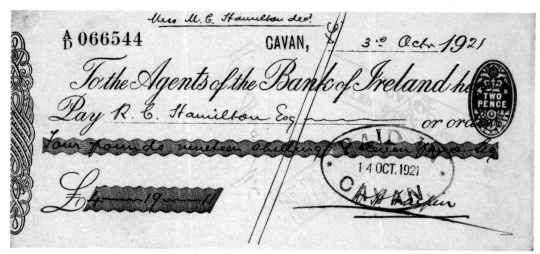

Fig. 129. To the Agents of the Bank of Ireland here, Cavan, 1921.

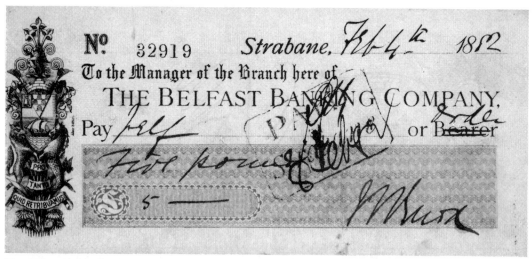

Fig. 130. The Belfast Banking Company, Strabane, 1882. *Part of the London Joint City & Midland Bank from 1917.*

Fig. 131. The Munster & Leinster Bank Limited, Waterford, 1896. *Merged into the Allied Irish Banks Limited in 1972.*

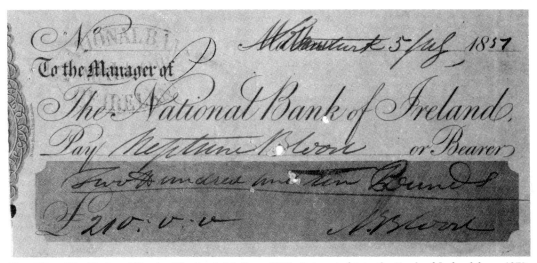

Fig. 132. The National Bank of Ireland, Mallow, 1851. *Integrated into the Bank of Ireland from 1972.*

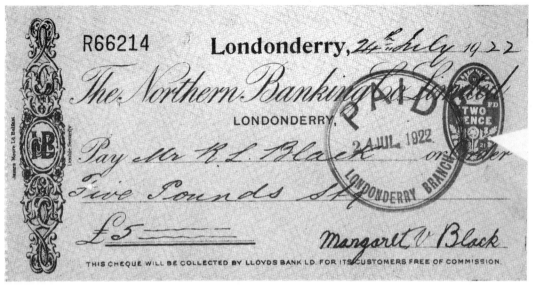

Fig. 133. The Northern Banking Company Limited, Londonderry, 1922.

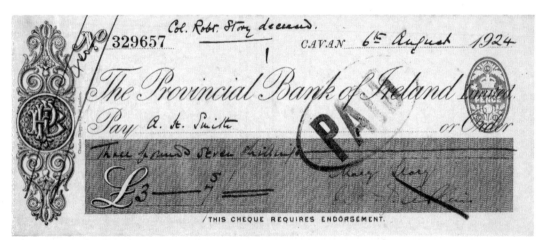

Fig. 134. The Provincial Bank of Ireland Limited, Cavan, 1924. *Another title which merged into the Allied Irish Banks Ltd, in 1972.*

Fig. 135. The Royal Bank of Ireland Limited, Dublin, 1914. *Yet another constituent for the Allied Irish Banks!.*

Fig. 136. To the Ulster Banking Company, Donegal, 1869. *Became part of the National Westminster Bank group from 1917.*

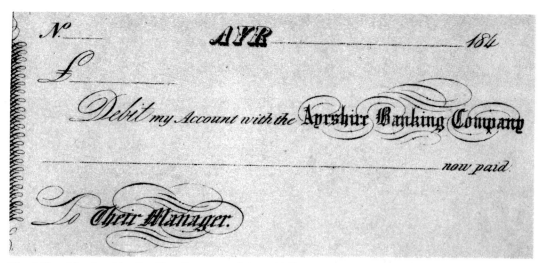

Fig. 137. The Ayrshire Banking Company, Ayr, c. 1840's. *Joined the Western Bank of Scotland in 1845.*

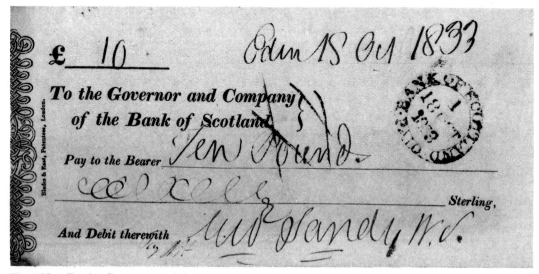

Fig. 138. To the Governor and Company of the Bank of Scotland, Edinburgh, 1833. *Scotland's most senior Bank, established 1695.*

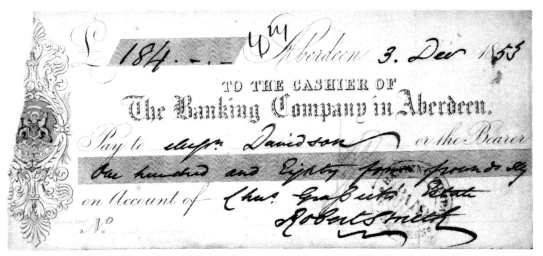

Fig. 139. To the Cashier of the Banking Company in Aberdeen, 1853. *Amalgamated with the Union Bank of Scotland in 1849.*

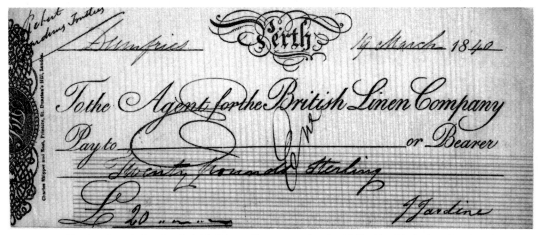

Fig. 140. To the Agent for the British Linen Company, Perth, 1840. *Established in 1746 in the Linen trade.*

Fig. 141. The Caledonian Banking Company Limited, 1901, an example from the Head Office at Inverness. *Passes to Bank of Scotland 1907.*

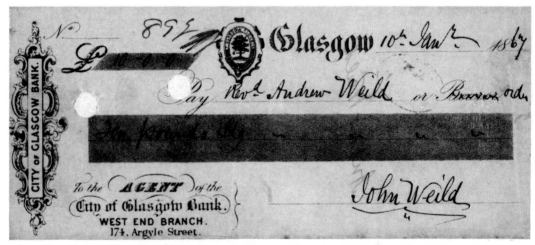

Fig. 142. City of Glasgow Bank, 174 Argyle Street, Glasgow, 1867. *Failed in 1878, Scotland's most famous Banking crash.*

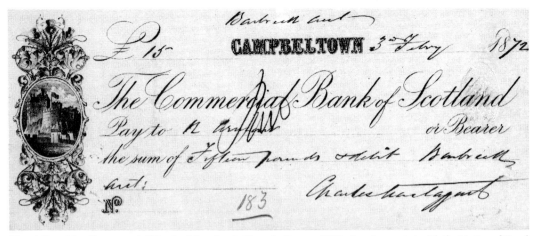

Fig. 143. The Commercial Bank of Scotland, Campbeltown, 1872. *Amalgamated with the National Bank of Scotland in 1959.*

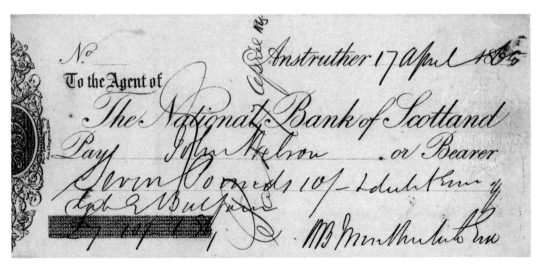

Fig. 144. To the Agent of the National Bank of Scotland, Anstruther, 1865.

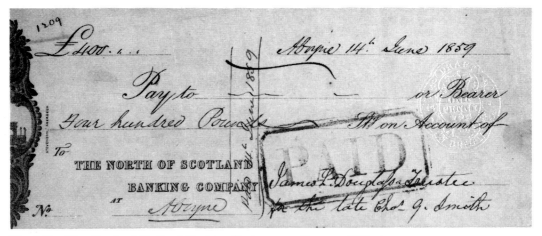

Fig. 145. The North of Scotland Banking Company at Aboyne, 1859.

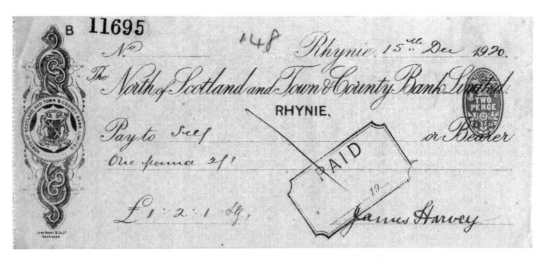

Fig. 146. Later to become The North of Scotland and Town & County Bank Limited. *This item from Rhynie is dated 1920.*

Fig. 147. The Royal Bank of Scotland, Elgin, 1883. *Another very old title going back as far as 1727.*

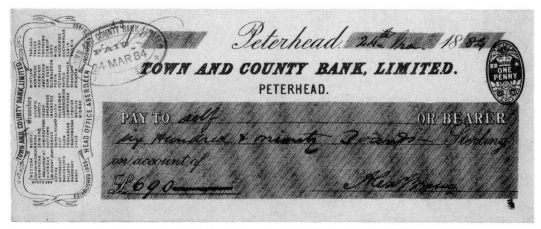

Fig. 148. Town and County Bank Limited, Peterhead, 1884. *See Fig. 146 following 1908 amalgamation with North of Scotland Bank.*

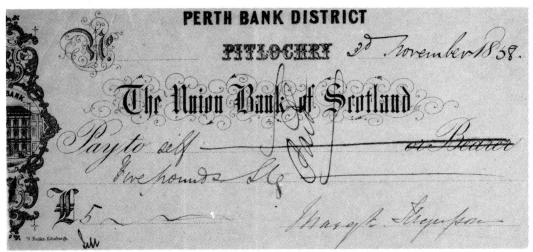

Fig. 149. The Union Bank of Scotland, Pitlochry, 1858. *Includes reference to original Perth Bank which it absorbed a year before.*

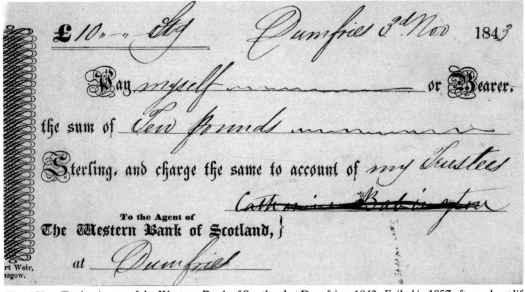

Fig. 150. To the Agent of the Western Bank of Scotland at Dumfries, 1843. *Failed in 1857 after a short life of 25 years.*

CURRENT PRICES FOR CHEQUES

Please bear in mind the simple fact that every collectable is governed by the 'supply and demand' factor and that no two Dealers are likely to grade or price the same item in an identical manner. It must also be pointed out that we are not yet in a position to say just which cheques are genuinely 'rare' — much more time is needed to establish true values, so do beware of paying vastly inflated prices for any particular item. A good rule of thumb may be to try to establish the size of the original Bank network as its cheques SHOULD generally have survived in proportion to the numbers once issued — not an infallible guide but worth thinking about. Finally I make the point that the ultimate price for any cheque is the well worn phrase 'what the next man will pay for it' — so buy with both eyes open, but be prepared to allow some degree of flexibility on the following range of prices —

20th Century — generally plentiful, priced from a few pence to about £2.00 per item.

1900-c.1856 — mostly available around £2.00 to £5.00 with more being asked for an outstanding example, a small Bank or certain Over-prints.

PRE-1856-1800 — with few exceptions much scarcer, generally now priced in the £5.00 to £15.00 range. The 1856 date is recognised as a milestone as all cheques were subject to 1d duty — a rate which was to remain until 1918 when it was increased to 2d.

1800-1700 — virtually all now very scarce, average around £20-£30 per item for late 18th century, upwards to £100 with each decade back to 1700.

Before 1700 — all rare to very rare and within the range of £100 + to present general limit of up to £300 for the 1660's.

THE BRITISH CHEQUE COLLECTORS' SOCIETY

All well established collecting hobbies have a National Organisation through which members may gain from their shared interest and it is to be hoped that cheque collecting will also find its way forward through the above Society. Originally formed in 1980 the Society has not found the easiest path to pick its way out of recession but from late 1984 things have once again began to show signs of life with the issue of regular newsletters. Both the Society and indeed the hobby itself are in their infancy when compared to numerous other interests and both would be transformed with the injection of modest numbers. For those who seek further information on the Society's activities we invite them to write, enclosing an SAE in first instance, to — John Purser, 71 Mile Lane, Cheylesmore, Coventry, CV3 5GB, England.

For most of the cheques in this book I have been content to provide merely one or two lines of historical information. A list of major works for some of Britain's main Banks is given on the following page and each of these will give the reader an enormous amount of detail and insight into just how each Bank of today developed from earliest times. Further reference can be made to a recent edition of 'The Bankers' Almanac and Year Book' which includes, among many other fascinating facts, a listing of Amalgamations, Absorptions and Liquidations of Banks in the United Kingdom from 1700 onwards.

Collectors are able to insist on a high standard of condition for the specimens added to their collections. It is possible to obtain items back to about the 1830's, possibly earlier, which are still more or less in 'ex cheque book condition'. For material before the early 1800's one may well have to lower one's hopes and accept what is available, up-grading as and when better items appear.

Prices for unused cheque forms tend to be a little higher than for the used items, again a re-instatement of 'supply and demand' and should be kept in mind when buying.

FOR FURTHER READING — Students interested in learning more of the fascinating histories of the major British Banks may be advised to seek any of the following volumes for further information. In addition more modern 'booklets' may be available and it is well worth checking with one's local Bank.

BARCLAYS — HISTORY OF BARCLAYS BANK LTD., by P Mathews & A Tuke, 1926, London.

MIDLAND — A HUNDRED YEARS OF JOINT STOCK BANKING, by W Crick & J Wadsworth, third edition 1958, London.

LLOYDS — LLOYDS BANK IN THE HISTORY OF ENGLISH BANKING, by R Sayers, 1957, Oxford.

NATIONAL PROVINCIAL — NATIONAL PROVINCIAL BANK, 1833-1933, by H Withers, 1933, London.

WESTMINSTER — THE WESTMINSTER BANK THROUGH A CENTURY, 1836-1936, by T Gregory, 1936, London, Vols. I & II.

MARTINS — FOUR CENTURIES OF BANKING, by G Chandler, Vol. I (1964) and Vol. II (1968).

IRELAND — THE EMERGENCE OF THE IRISH BANKING SYSTEM, 1820-45, by G Barrow, 1975, Dublin.

SCOTLAND — SCOTTISH BANKING: A HISTORY 1695-1973, by Prof S. Checkland, 1975, Glasgow.

SCOTLAND — THE SCOTTISH PROVINCIAL BANKING COMPANIES 1747-1864, by C Munn, 1981, Edinburgh.

(The latter volume covers the Private Bankers in great depth).